BLESSED FAMILIES

BLESSED FAMILIES

ROBERT MORRIS

STUDY GUIDE

Blessed Families Study Guide
Copyright © 2019 by Robert Morris

Content taken from sermons delivered in 2019 by Robert Morris at Gateway Church, Southlake, TX.

ISBN: 978-1-949399-55-4

We hope you hear from the Holy Spirit and receive God's richest blessings from this book by Gateway Press. We want to provide the highest quality resources that take the messages, music, and media of Gateway Church to the world. For more information on other resources from Gateway Publishing®, go to gatewaypublishing.com.

Gateway Press, an imprint of Gateway Publishing
700 Blessed Way
Southlake, Texas 76092
gatewaypublishing.com

Printed in the United States of America
19 20 21 22 23   5 4 3 2 1

CONTENTS

THE BROKEN FAMILY

The spiritual characteristics and genetic tendencies from Adam and Eve have been passed on to us through the curse of the Fall. But Jesus came to redeem us from the curse!

ENGAGE
If you could direct a movie, what would the title and main plot be?

WATCH
Watch "The Broken Family."
- Think about how Satan got Adam and Eve to doubt their God-given identities.
- Look for the solution to our shame, blame, and fame problem.

(If you are not able to watch this teaching on video, read the following. Otherwise, skip to the **Talk** section after viewing.)

READ

We all come from a broken family. Even if you came from a Christian home, your parents were still broken. We're all broken because we all come from the first broken family—Adam and Eve.

We all have biological DNA and genetic characteristics that come from Adam and Eve. We also inherited spiritual DNA from them. I'm going to share with you the three results of the Fall.

Before the Fall, every person on Earth was in a perfect relationship with God and each other. But only a few verses later in the book of Genesis, everyone on Earth was in a broken relationship with God and each other.

Genesis 3:1 says,

> Now the serpent was more cunning than any beast of the field which the Lord God had made. And he said to the woman, "Has God indeed said, 'You shall not eat of every tree of the garden'?"

To get someone to sin, the first thing Satan did was cast doubt on the Word of God.

Genesis 3:2–6 goes on to say,

> And the woman said to the serpent, "We may eat the fruit of the trees of the garden; but of the fruit of the tree which *is* in the midst of the garden, God has said, 'You shall not eat it, nor shall you touch it, lest you die.'"

Then the serpent said to the woman, "You will not surely
die. For God knows that in the day you eat of it your eyes will be
opened, and you will be like God, knowing good and evil."

So when the woman saw that the tree *was* good for food, that it *was*
pleasant to the eyes, and a tree desirable to make *one* wise, she took of
its fruit and ate. She also gave to her husband with her, and he ate.

Adam was with Eve while the devil was talking to her, but he never
did anything about it. The Fall of mankind cannot be fully blamed
on a female. Both man and woman sinned against God.

There are three things Eve saw in the fruit. First John 2:16 says
there are three things in the world: "The lust of the flesh, the lust of
the eyes, and the pride of life." The lust of the flesh represents Eve's
eyeing the fruit and seeing it was good for food. The lust of the eyes
was Eve's noticing the fruit was pleasant to look at. And the pride of
life was Eve's belief that the fruit from the tree could make her wise.

Three things entered the world at the Fall that still affect us to
this day:

Shame

Adam and Eve hid from God in shame after they sinned.
Genesis 3:7–11 says,

Then the eyes of both of them were opened, and they knew that
they *were* naked; and they sewed fig leaves together and made
themselves coverings.

> And they heard the sound of the Lord God walking in
> the garden in the cool of the day, and Adam and his wife hid
> themselves from the presence of the Lord God among the trees of
> the garden.
> Then the Lord God called to Adam and said to him, "Where
> *are* you?"
> So he said, "I heard Your voice in the garden, and I was afraid
> because I was naked; and I hid myself."
> And He said, "Who told you that you *were* naked?"

Adam had fear because he had shame. No one had to tell him he was naked. Shame immediately entered the world when sin entered. Adam and Eve were hiding from God and each other.

Genesis 3:21 says, "For Adam and his wife the Lord God made tunics of skin, and clothed them." God made clothes for Adam and Eve from animal skin. He had to shed blood to make coverings for them until His plan to cover mankind forever in Jesus' blood was complete.

Revelation 3:18 says, "I counsel you to buy from Me gold refined in the fire, that you may be rich; and white garments, that you may be clothed, *that* the shame of your nakedness may not be revealed." Gold represents God's Word. The Bible says His Word is more precious than silver. God is not referring to real clothes but to a spiritual covering for shame. Isaiah 61:10 says, "For He has clothed me with the garments of salvation, / He has covered me with the robe of righteousness."

The only thing that will cover shame is righteousness. Righteousness means "right standing with God." The only way to take care of your sin and shame is to be in a right relationship with God, and the only way to be in a right relationship with Him is through Jesus Christ. Sometimes we think, *If I can just overcome this, if I can start living better, if I can stop falling in this or that sin, then I won't have shame.* We should live righteously, but that in itself will not remove our shame. Only Jesus Christ can remove our shame.

When we believe in Jesus, He moves our shame, guilt, and sin out of our account and deposits His righteousness instead. Romans 4:3 says, "Abraham believed God, and it was accounted to him for righteousness." God does the same for us.

When Jesus went to the cross, the sin of everyone in the whole world was taken out of their account and put in Jesus' account. Then He died as the sacrifice for those sins. He died for everyone, but not everyone is saved because not everyone has believed. It's only when you believe that righteousness is put in your account. God's already taken care of your sin; you just need to believe in Jesus.

The problem, I've noticed, is that I still sin even though I've been saved. So has every other human being on this earth who has given their life to Jesus. Satan wants you to believe you're worse than other people, but we've all sinned. The only way to overcome shame is to believe God has deposited Jesus' righteousness in your account.

Blame

> And He said, "Who told you that you *were* naked? Have you eaten
> from the tree of which I commanded you that you should not eat?"
> Then the man said, "The woman whom You gave *to be* with me,
> she gave me of the tree, and I ate."
> And the Lord God said to the woman, "What *is* this you have
> done?"
> The woman said, "The serpent deceived me, and I ate"
> (Genesis 3:11–13).

We inherited blame from Adam and Eve, our spiritual parents.
Most of the time, we'll say one of two things: "It's not my fault"
or "It's all my fault." Both these mindsets are wrong. In both
instances, we are trying to put blame somewhere. This is a result
of the Fall.

Think about how many people live in bitterness toward others or
toward God. They think things like, *My boss didn't promote me. I read*
The Blessed Life, *but God hasn't blessed me. Apparently something's
wrong with me.* Don't live with blame! It comes from a person
named Satan.

The other word for blame is "accuse." Satan is the accuser.
Revelation 12:10 says,

> Then I heard a loud voice saying in heaven, "Now salvation, and
> strength, and the kingdom of our God, and the power of His Christ

have come, for the accuser of our brethren, who accused them
before our God day and night, has been cast down."

Before you accuse someone, you need to realize that person
is your brother or your sister. They're your "brethren." When you
accuse someone else, you're acting like Satan. We need more love
and forgiveness in the body of Christ.

Fame

This isn't referring to being famous but rather wanting to be
recognized. It's that insecurity we all have that causes us to need
recognition.

In verses 14 and 15 of Genesis 3, God announces the curse
that came on the serpent because of what he did. In verse 16, He
announces the curse that came on Eve. And in verses 17-19, He
announces the curse that came on Adam. When it comes to these
verses, I want you to get your theology straight—God Himself did
not curse them; instead, He told them about the curse they had
brought on themselves. He had warned them that they would die.
He was telling them how death had resulted from what they did.

Christ came to redeem us from those curses, but unfortunately,
some people are still living under them.

Soon after that, "Adam called his wife's name Eve, because she
was the mother of all living" (Genesis 3:20). You may not think that
to be such a bad thing. After all, the name *Eve* means "life." But
God did not give her this name.

At the end of Genesis 2, Adam said of Eve, "This *is* now bone of my bones / and flesh of my flesh" (v. 23). He was saying she was part of him and that they were one entity. Immediately after the Fall, Adam labeled Eve as separate and distinct from him, saying her purpose was to bear children (being "the mother of all living").

Before the Fall, God had never called her "Eve." In the King James Version, Genesis 5:2 says, "Male and female created he them; and blessed them, and called their name Adam, in the day when they were created." In the Hebrew, *Adam* means 'mankind.' Some people think it means man, but it refers to mankind, both male and female. Genesis 5:2 (NKJV) says, "He created them male and female, and blessed them and called them Mankind in the day they were created."

The Bible says God makes the two one, and "what God has joined together, let not man separate" (Mark 10:9). As soon as sin came into the world, Adam declared himself separate from Eve. He labeled her and told her that childbearing was her purpose. Ladies have been struggling with this ever since. Many women wonder, "Is my only purpose to be a mother?"

I've actually said in the past that a man's highest calling is to be a husband and father and a woman's highest calling is to be a wife and mother. I no longer believe that. Our highest calling is to be a child—a child of God. If you're a good child of God, you'll be a good husband and father or a good wife and mother. This is why some women suffer from depression when their children move out—they think their purpose has been fulfilled and their calling is over.

Each person has a calling. And every person has a gift from God. You need to know what your purpose is because that will fulfill you.

When Adam labeled Eve, there began a separation and competition between husbands and wives. This spread to their children as well. In Genesis 4, Abel was noticed for his offering, and Cain was not. There was a competition between them, and Cain eventually killed Abel because of it.

You can see a spirit of competition in your own children. They want to be noticed and recognized. And in an effort to be separate, sometimes they rebel, because they're tired of being known as part of a family; they want to be known as a unique individual. This can happen when they hear things like, "Aren't you so-and-so's boy?" "Your sister was valedictorian. Are you smart too?" or "Are you as good at football as your older brother?" Each child wants to be recognized for their own gifts and talents.

The lie of the Fall says you need to be known for something and be an individual, but the truth is you are an individual, created to be like God.

The answer for all the shame, blame, and fame is Jesus Christ. Acts 3 talks about the seed of Abraham: Jesus. Verse 25 says, "And in your seed all the families of the earth shall be blessed." We not only put our trust in Jesus for salvation, but we also continue to trust Him to take away the shame, blame, and fame.

There's a hymn written by William Cowper. He had been a very immoral man and was miraculously saved. God began to bless him and help get his life in order. William had an opportunity to serve as a clerk in the House of Lords, but he wanted to back out after he learned he had to go through a public examination before he could serve.

He was afraid his past would be revealed, and he got so discouraged about it that he tried to kill himself four times. At first, he thought to jump off a bridge, but he was too afraid of heights. Then he bought some poison for himself but dropped and broke the bottle before he got it home. Third, he tried to hang himself from a beam in his house, but the beam broke when he jumped. Lastly, he tried to stab himself with a knife, but the knife blade broke as well.

He became so exhausted with all his suicide attempts that he fell asleep. When he woke up, the words to this hymn were in his mind, and he wrote them down. He decided to go to the public examination. He told everyone about his past and how Jesus had forgiven him, and many people accepted Christ at the House of Lords because of William's testimony.

These are the words he wrote when he woke up:

There is a fountain filled with blood
Drawn from Immanuel's veins;
And sinners, plunged beneath that flood,
Lose all their guilty stains:
Lose all their guilty stains,
Lose all their guilty stains;
And sinners, plunged beneath that flood,
Lose all their guilty stains.

NOTES

_____

_____

_____

_____

_____

_____

TALK

These questions can be used for group discussion or personal reflection.

Question 1

According to Isaiah 61:10 and Romans 4:3, what does God do for us when we believe in Him?

_____

_____

_____

_____

Question 2

Ask the Holy Spirit if you are still carrying shame as a result of your sins. What's the only thing that can cover your shame?

_____

_____

_____

_____

Question 3
If Jesus came to redeem us from the curse of sin, why do some people continue to live under that curse?

_____

_____

_____

_____

Question 4
How was Eve labeled when Adam gave her a new name?

_____

_____

_____

_____

Question 5
What lie did Adam and Eve believe when they chose to sin and eat the forbidden fruit? What was the truth?

_____

_____

_____

_____

PRAY

If studying alone, ask the Holy Spirit to reveal the truth about Himself to you. If in a group, take some time to pray for each other as you think about the truths discussed in this session.

EXPLORE

Do you want to go deeper with this teaching? Here are some additional things to think about, pray for, or write about in your journal throughout the next week.

Key Quote

> *The lie of the Fall says you need to be known for something and be an individual, but the truth is you are an individual, created to be like God.*

Do you feel pressure to stand out in a special way? How does knowing you are already uniquely created help relieve that pressure?

_____

_____

_____

_____

_____

Key Verses

Genesis 3; Isaiah 61:10; Revelation 3:18, 12:10

What truths stand out to you as you read these verses?

_____

_____

_____

What is the Holy Spirit saying to you through these Scriptures?

_____

_____

_____

Key Question

According to Genesis 1:27, what belief can help us recognize and reject the lies Adam and Eve believed?

Key Prayer

Father God, help me find my secure identity in You as Your child. Lord Jesus, thank You for taking all my sin and shame with You when You died on the cross. Holy Spirit, reveal parts of my heart that still want to be validated by men or tend to blame others for my problems. Help me bring my problems to You and trust You for the solution. In Jesus' name, Amen.

THE BLESSED MARRIAGE

Marriage represents God's image on earth, Christ and the Church, and the covenant God makes with His beloved children.

ENGAGE

Share a time that you dreaded a change, but it ended up being for good.

WATCH

Watch "The Blessed Marriage."

- Think about the example a godly marriage sets for nonbelievers.
- Look for why marriage is so important to God.

(If you are not able to watch this teaching on video, read the following. Otherwise, skip to the **Talk** section after viewing.)

READ

Marriage is under attack in our country and all over the world. In 1930, 83% of adult Americans were married. Today, only 49.7% are married. I want to share with you why Satan hates marriage so much. I'm also going to show you a passage from Matthew 19 that I believe to be the most in-depth passage on marriage in the Bible. Most would believe it's Ephesians 5, and Ephesians 5 is an extremely important chapter on marriage. However, in Matthew 19, there's a question asked about marriage and divorce, and Jesus Himself gives the answer. Remember: Jesus is God. This is *God's* answer concerning marriage and divorce!

I also want to say that if you've ever experienced divorce, in no way do I want you to feel condemnation. A marriage takes two people. If not for the grace of God and my wife Debbie, we would be divorced. She could have divorced me on several occasions because in my twenties, I was a jerk and a chauvinist. I verbally abused her, and I said and did stupid things. It's by God's grace and the grace given to me by Debbie that we are not divorced. So this is a no-condemnation message.

I want to show you what the Bible says about marriage and divorce and how important marriage is in the Bible. Personally, I don't think people realize how serious God is about marriage. I want to show you why. God Himself gives us the reason marriage is so important.

Matthew 19:3 says, "The Pharisees also came to Him, testing Him, and saying to Him, 'Is it lawful for a man to divorce his wife for *just* any reason?'" The word *just* in any Bible version you read is italicized in this verse. When you see a word italicized in the Bible, it means it's not in the original language but translators added it to help us understand the passage better. So what the Pharisees are really asking is, "Is it lawful for a man to divorce his wife for any reason?" The Greek word for *any* is an exclusive Greek word which means 'any reason at all.' In other words, they're asking God if it's lawful to divorce for any reason at all.

Jesus answered them in Matthew 19:4-5, "Have you not read that He who made them at the beginning 'made them male and female,' and said, 'For this reason a man shall leave his father and mother and be joined to his wife, and the two shall become one flesh'?"

In other words, Jesus says, "Are you crazy? Have you not read the Bible yourself? If you'd have read the Bible, you wouldn't need to ask Me this question." The word *joined* in this passage is the same word you use when you yoke animals together. And it means equally yoked, with each person doing his or her share. That's the only way marriage works. I've heard someone say marriage is 50/50. It's not—it's 100/100. It takes 100% commitment from both sides.

Jesus doesn't exaggerate. He doesn't lie or stretch the truth. He says, "The two become one." Matthew 19:6 says, "So then, they are no longer two but one flesh. Therefore what God has joined together, let not man separate."

Whenever I see the word *therefore* in Scripture, I have to stop and ask myself what it's "there for." This is the answer to the question they asked. They asked if it was lawful to divorce. Jesus said, "Let not any man separate what God has joined together." Jesus' answer is "No."

Then the Pharisees asked another question: "Why then did Moses command to give a certificate of divorce, and to put her away?" (v. 7). Jesus replied, "Moses, because of the hardness of your hearts, permitted you to divorce your wives, but from the beginning it was not so" (v. 8).

I'm going to speak the truth now. Please hear me. I'm not trying to attack someone if they've experienced this. In every divorce, there is at least one person with a hard heart. Sometimes there are two, but most times there's really just one.

The Pharisees said Moses *commanded* they give a certificate of divorce. But Jesus says Moses only *permitted* them to divorce if they had a hard heart. When this came to be part of the law in Moses' time, a man would marry more than one woman and neglect his first wife—abusing her, letting other men abuse her, and not letting her go free. So Moses made it part of the law that a husband must let that woman go free so another man could marry her and treat her like the queen she really was.

I want you to notice something: Moses represents the law, and Jesus represents grace. John 1:17 says, "For the law was given through Moses, *but* grace and truth came through Jesus Christ." Here's my point: Jesus said divorce is not lawful. We would think it would be the opposite, that the law says you can't divorce, but grace says it's okay. But grace says, "You're in a covenant. You work things out," and law says, "You've got a hard heart, so let her go."

Here are three things you need to know about a blessed marriage:

Marriage Represents God

In Matthew 19:4-5, Jesus says, "Have you not read that He who made *them* at the beginning 'made them male and female,' and said, 'For this reason a man shall leave his father and mother and be joined to his wife, and the two shall become one flesh'?"

Now go back to Genesis 1:26-27:

> Then God said, "Let Us make man in Our image, according to Our likeness; let them have dominion over the fish of the sea, over the birds of the air, and over the cattle, over all the earth and over every creeping thing that creeps on the earth." So God created man in His *own* image; in the image of God He created him; male and female He created them.

God is a triune, three-in-one God (Father, Son, and Holy Spirit). And remember that the word *man* in these verses means *mankind*. Male *and* female is the image of God. But not just any man or any woman—a husband and a wife. When God wanted to create a portrait of Himself on this earth, He created marriage.

Satan hates marriage because it's the image of God on this earth. Satan did not attack Adam when Adam was alone. He didn't attack until the image of God appeared on the earth. That's when he got scared. He wasn't scared of one man by himself—he was scared when God's image showed up. Satan didn't see God in just Adam—he saw God in Adam *and* Eve together.

God is a triune God. That means He is three in one. If you see God, you see one God, but if you look closely, you see three persons who make up God. God made mankind in His image; a marriage is a husband, a wife, and God—three in one! That is a blessed marriage and the only way marriage works.

When a lost couple comes into our home, they should leave with a lot of questions. They should say, "That's amazing. I saw something I can't really explain but I'm going to try to. I saw two individuals, yet it seemed like they were just one. They were completely different persons, but because there was so much unity between them, it seemed like they were one."

The blessed marriage is one made up of unity and equality with order, but the world knows nothing of that. The world says, "If one's the leader, how can you be equal?" That's never been a problem with God—there's God the Father, God the Son, and God the Holy Spirit, but God the Father is the leader. If you think about a couple ballroom dancing, they are moving in complete harmony and unity. But if you talk to any dance instructor, they'll tell you one of them is leading.

If you're single and wondering how you can represent God on this earth, look at Jesus. He represented God and was single for 33 years.

Marriage Represents Christ and the Church

Now we're going to look at what Ephesians 5 says about marriage. Watch what three words it starts with and what verse from Genesis it quotes.

> For this reason a man shall leave his father and mother and be
> joined to his wife, and the two shall become one flesh. This is
> a great mystery, but I speak concerning Christ and the Church.
> Nevertheless let each one of you in particular so love his own
> wife as himself, and let the wife *see* that she respects *her*
> husband (v. 31–33).

Husband and wife together represent the Trinity, but as a man, you represent Christ, and as a woman, you represent the Church.

Husbands, when you're trying to win a friend to the Lord, show him how Jesus will treat him by how you treat your wife. If you talk down to her, abuse her, or order her around, others won't want to follow the Jesus you're representing. But if you love your wife, honor her, and treat her like royalty, in so doing, you'll be rightfully representing Jesus Christ to those around you.

Wives, let's say your friend tells you she doesn't really know how to pray. You should be able to tell her, "Well, I just talk to the Lord the same way I talk to my husband." If you're respectful and honoring of him even when he's not around, you are representing the Church well on this earth. But if you use foul language with him, yell at him, or belittle him, you are an ill representation of Christ's Church on earth.

Marriage Represents Covenant

Are you noticing how important marriage is to God? It's His image on the earth, it represents Christ and the Church, and it represents covenant.

In Malachi, God tells the people why He's not accepting their offerings: their faith, family, and finances are out of order. After God tells the people this, He says through His prophet:

> "Yet you say, 'For what reason?'
> Because the Lord has been witness
> Between you and the wife of your youth,
> With whom you have dealt treacherously.
> Yet she is your companion
> and your wife by covenant" (Malachi 2:14).

I love Jimmy Evans' definition of the difference between a covenant and a contract— "In a contract, we protect our rights, and we limit our responsibilities. In covenant, we give up our rights, and we pick up our responsibilities." This is the example to the world. If a lost person asks, "How can I know that God will keep His word to me?" we should say, "Look at how my wife and I have kept our word" (because we entered into a covenant too).

Let me remind you of the covenant you entered into if you're married. It's for richer or for poorer, in sickness and in health, for better or for worse, until death do us part. It's an example of the new covenant.

Let me explain the difference between the old Mosaic covenant and the new Abrahamic covenant (based on faith). In the Mosaic covenant, God told Israel they had a part and He had a part in the covenant. God's part was to protect, provide for, and bless them. He would be their Father and love them. Israel's part was to follow the law completely. Israel said, "Okay! We'll do it." But they were breaking their covenant even before Moses got off the mountain where God gave it to him.

You may wonder, *Why did God even bother with this covenant?* One reason was to show His standard of moral perfection. The second reason (you can find in Romans and Galatians) was to frustrate us to come to Christ. And if you don't think you'd get frustrated, read Leviticus. There's a whole chapter on what you're required to do if you get a scab!

God never wanted a legalistic relationship—He always wanted a love relationship. He wanted us to get so frustrated that we'd finally say, "God, I just want to have a relationship with You," and He'd say, "Great, that's all I've wanted all along."

In the new covenant, God told Jesus, "They aren't going to be able to keep the covenant, so would you be willing to go to earth and fulfill the covenant they can't keep and die the death they should die?" Jesus said, "Ok, I'll do it." The Father asks us,

"Can you believe that Jesus lived the life you couldn't live and died the death you should've died?" All we have to do to keep this covenant is say, "Yes, Lord, I believe." Then He makes us His children and says He will never leave nor forsake us. That's what marriage is—even if my spouse doesn't keep their end of the covenant, I'll keep my end. We're telling the world, "This is what God is like." He's a covenant-keeping God.

NOTES

_____

_____

_____

_____

_____

_____

TALK

These questions can be used for group discussion or personal reflection.

Question 1

In Matthew 19, how does Jesus respond to the Pharisees' question?

_____

_____

_____

_____

Question 2

As a child, what were you taught about marriage and divorce? How did Pastor Robert's message challenge and/or surprise you?

_____

_____

_____

_____

Question 3
How can marriage attract or repel unbelievers when it comes to Christ?

_____

_____

_____

_____

Question 4
Why does Satan hate marriage so much?

_____

_____

_____

_____

Question 5
Ask the Holy Spirit, "Does my relationship with Jesus represent God to others?"

_____

_____

_____

_____

PRAY

If studying alone, ask the Holy Spirit to reveal the truth about Himself to you. If in a group, take some time to pray for each other as you think about the truths discussed in this session.

EXPLORE

Do you want to go deeper with this teaching? Here are some additional things to think about, pray for, or write about in your journal throughout the next week.

Key Quote

When God wanted to create a portrait of Himself on this earth, He created marriage.

How does marriage reflect the Trinity?

_____

_____

_____

_____

_____

Key Verses

Matthew 19:3-8; Genesis 1:26-27; Ephesians 5:31-33; Malachi 2:14
What truths stand out to you as you read these verses?

_____

_____

_____

What is the Holy Spirit saying to you through these Scriptures?

_____

_____

_____

Key Question

How can God use you to reflect His image and character to the unbelievers in your life?

Key Prayer

Father God, thank You for the truth in Your Word. Help me
see, hear, and believe it in my heart today. Jesus, thank You for
keeping Your covenant with me even when I've been unfaithful.
Holy Spirit, help me continually grow into the likeness of Jesus
and faithfully represent the love of the Father to those around me.
In Jesus' name, Amen.

3

FROM BROKEN TO BLESSED

We all came from Adam and Eve—a broken family—but God wants us to go from broken to blessed.

ENGAGE

What outdoor activities do you enjoy? When have you seen or experienced evidence of God in nature?

WATCH

Watch "From Broken to Blessed."
- Think about what stage you're in.
- Look for what it's like to have a mature relationship with God.

(If you are not able to watch this teaching on video, read the following. Otherwise, skip to the **Talk** section after viewing.)

READ

We all came from a broken family—Adam and Eve. "Broken" isn't referring to divorce but the brokenness of *sin*. I want us to look at the story of the prodigal son and see the four stages we all go through when we move from broken to blessed.

Give me.

Every baby, every spiritual baby, and every marriage starts at this stage. We can see this stage in Luke 15:12: "And the younger of them said to *his* father, 'Father, give me the portion of goods that falls to *me*.'"

As parents, we desire for our children to grow out of the "give me" stage. As spiritual babies, when we're born again, we also start in this stage. God doesn't resent that, just as we don't resent it when our baby needs milk. We don't expect anything different from that baby, and in the same way, God isn't upset that we start out in the "give me" stage.

If you think about it, many of us get saved out of selfishness. We get saved because we don't want to go to hell or because we want God to clean up the mess we've made. God isn't upset about this, but He does want us to grow up.

It's the same with marriage. The husband wants the wife to meet his needs, and the wife wants the husband to meet her needs. There are some needs God has designed a husband and a wife to meet for each other, but there are some needs only God can meet.

If you're looking to your spouse to meet the needs only God can meet, you're going to be disappointed.

Let me show you another famous "give me" passage in Scripture. Matthew 26:14-15 says, "Then one of the twelve, called Judas Iscariot, went to the chief priests and said, 'What are you willing to give me if I deliver Him to you?' And they counted out to him thirty pieces of silver."

Give me. That's where we all start. Debbie and I have grandchildren, and we love them. They're maturing and growing, but they're still children, so they're in the "give me" stage. We love to spend time with our grandchildren, but here's what I've noticed about them—we never get to do what I want to do! They never say to me, "Papaw, you're such a good papaw. What would you like to do today?" They tell me what they want to do. I've seen Frozen 3,472 times!

Use Me

Next is the "use me" stage. There is a "use me" that comes from a mature standpoint, and we'll talk about that later on, but this particular "use me" is different. It's "Use me so I can be seen or significant (or feel important)." This is the next stage that every Christian goes through.

We say, "Give me" because of selfishness; we say, "Use me" because of selfish ambition. Philippians 2:3 says, "*Let* nothing *be done* through selfish ambition or conceit, but in lowliness of mind let each esteem others better than himself." In the English, "selfish ambition" is two words, but in the Greek it's one word. It's in the New Testament seven times. Sometimes it translates to self-seeking. James 3:14 says, "But if you have bitter envy and self-seeking in your hearts, do not boast and lie against the truth."

Here's the point: When the Bible talks about ambition, it puts the word "selfish" in front of it. Some may ask, "Isn't there a good ambition?" According to the Bible, there isn't. The definition of ambition is "self-seeking, self-promoting." You may say, "Well, what if they have drive?" That's great. But why do they have drive? When I'm training up men and women in ministry, I'm trying to beat selfish ambition out of them. I know it's there. Every person is born with it.

I can show you this in a verse about Simon the magician. He sees the laying on of hands and the giving of the Holy Spirit from Peter and John and says to them in Acts 8:19, "Give me this power also, that anyone on whom I lay hands may receive the Holy Spirit." In other words, he was saying, "Give me something so I can feel significant and have power."

Let's relate this to marriage now. We start out saying, "Give me something so I'll feel good about myself and be happy." Then we move into, "You're not meeting my needs or making me happy, so I need to do something to make myself happy." Most of the marriage counseling I've done fits into these two stages. The second stage (I need to do something) is normally when divorce occurs. That person is trying to do something to get happiness, but happiness does not come from something. It only comes from Someone—His name is Jesus.

In the prodigal son's life, he left in the second stage to do something that he thought would make him happy. Luke 15:13 says, "And not many days after, the younger son gathered all together, journeyed to a far country, and there wasted his possessions with prodigal living." *Prodigal* here means sexually immoral.

I'm going to say something that may shock you now: *God did not create marriage to make you happy.* Some of you are thinking, "It's working!" Here's another shock: *God created marriage to kill you.* In essence, yes, He created marriage to make you happy, but He knows the only way you'll ever be happy is if you die to self.

Personally, I think God said to Himself, "How can we get Adam to die to self? I know—let's make him live with someone who's completely opposite of himself. And if that doesn't work, we'll give him children."

Search Me

We begin to mature in this stage. In Luke 15:17, it says of the prodigal son, "But when he came to himself." He matured when he began to search his own heart.

In Psalm 139:23–24 (KJV), the psalmist puts it this way:

Search me, O God, and know my heart: try me, and know my thoughts:
And see if there be any wicked way in me, and lead me in the way everlasting.

This is when we stop focusing on someone else meeting our needs or what's wrong with our spouse and start focusing on what's wrong with *ourselves*. Until we begin asking God to fix us instead of asking Him to fix others around us, we are immature believers. The maturation process requires we move from "give me" and "use me" to *search me*.

When you genuinely ask God to search you and ask Him to reveal what's wrong in your own heart, you've begun the maturation stage. If you really want a blessed family and a blessed marriage, fix yourself; work on yourself. Let God take care of others' growth.

One time I was talking to the Lord and complaining saying, "But Lord, did you see what she did?" He said to me, "No. I was just looking at you." He gave me a vision I'd like to share. Think about God taking a large tube and putting it over you, watching you and everything you do. Then He sees you throw a fit. He's not concerned with whatever caused you to throw the fit. He's concerned with your attitudes and actions, no matter the outside circumstances. I'm not responsible for anyone else's actions—I'm only responsible for my actions and my reactions.

Think about if God put the tube over His Son, Jesus. God could've put the tube over Jesus, and He would've been pleased with every action and every reaction—even when people nailed Jesus to the cross! God looked through the tube and saw Jesus say, "Father, please forgive them."

I started thinking about the word *search*. My son James went through a stage when he was about two or three years old in which he liked to hide, and he got very good at it. Some children hide but are still visible to you. Or they giggle when you come in the room. But James never giggled. He was crazy quiet. He could hide so well it scared us. I'd have to go in room after room and say, "James, I'm not playing anymore. If you don't come out right now, I'm going to spank you." He still didn't come out! One time, we searched for him for over an hour. I got in the car and drove around the neighborhood looking for him. We were about to call the police when I prayed, "Lord, You have to help me find James." At that moment, I remembered a lean-to I'd built for my lawnmower. I had already looked there but hadn't looked very far in. I'd only looked far enough to see the lawnmower. I went back and bent way down to look in, and I could see him sitting on the lawnmower. I looked in at him, and he said to me, "I hide good." I wanted to say, "And I spank good," but I was so happy to see him that I didn't spank him.

We used to have to search diligently for James when he hid. If you've ever lost a child in the mall or some place, you know how diligently you searched for them until they were found. Here's my question to you: how diligently are you searching your own heart? That's what David said—"Search my heart, try me, know my thoughts and see if there's any wicked way in me." That's a sign of maturity.

Make Me

The fourth stage going from broken to blessed is "make me." We start with "give me." We move to "use me," but it's for the wrong reason. We then say, "God, search me. I want to have purity on the inside." Then we move on to say, "Make me a vessel fit for the Master's use." If we say it another way, we can say, "Make me a servant to my spouse, my family, to the church, and to You."

In Luke 15:19, the prodigal son decides to tell his father, "I am no longer worthy to be called your son. Make me like one of your hired servants." I think he's actually saying, "I know I'm your son, but make me your servant. I want a servant's heart and attitude."

Sometimes when we talk about the prodigal son, we have a tendency to say, "That doesn't relate to me; I've never gone into sin like that." But remember this father had two sons. Did you know both sons had the same attitude? The younger son told his father, "Give me." Here's what the older son said to his father in Luke 15:29—"These many years I have been serving you; I never transgressed your commandment at any time; and yet you never gave me a young goat, that I might make merry with my friends.'" The father responds in verse 31, saying, "Son, you are always with me, and all that I have is yours." The answer to the maturation process and "give me" attitude is this: God says, "It's not what I can give you—it's that you can be with Me. And when you're with Me, everything I have is yours."

There's a Hebrew word and a Greek word for blessed. The Greek word is *makarios*. It means happy. When we talk about being blessed, it simply means being happy. Some people actually feel guilty when God starts blessing them because they come from such a brokenness that they don't feel worthy. The truth is, we aren't worthy—but we believe in Jesus who is worthy. And Father God wants to bless you, just as you want to bless your kids. The act of blessing has nothing to do with you or your performance—it has to do with His nature and who He is.

I started thinking about the word *blessed* and the word m*akarios*, and I'd like to share a testimony I heard. Pastor Jack Hayford was walking around his neighborhood and remembered a golden Labrador retriever he'd previously had. He thought, *I'd like to have a golden Lab to go on walks with me.* He only thought about it for that one moment and then went on with his day. A few days later, he and his wife, Anna, were driving to their vacation home, and as they came over a hill, they saw a man leaving his dog by the side of the road. They and another woman stopped and agreed that it looked like the man was abandoning the dog. As Jack walked up to the dog, the dog wagged his tail and looked as if he had a smile on his face. So Jack called him Mack, short for Makarios. Jack and his wife took the dog with them so they could find the owner and call shelters to see if anyone was looking for the dog. No one claimed the dog (which happened to be a golden Lab), so they decided the dog was a gift from the Lord. Later, Jack was walking with his new dog and came to the same place where he'd thought, *I'd like to have a golden Lab to walk with me*, and remembered when he'd had that thought just a few weeks before. Then he thought, *Why would I* *think God would arrange all those details just so I could have this dog?* As soon as he thought it, the Lord told him, "Why wouldn't I?"

Quit thinking, *Why would God want to bless me?* And start thinking, *Why wouldn't God want to bless me?* He sent His own Son to die for us. Why wouldn't He want to bless our families and take us from broken to blessed? He's a good God.

NOTES

_____

_____

_____

_____

_____

_____

TALK

These questions can be used for group discussion or personal reflection.

Question 1
In what stage does every person begin? How does God feel about this stage?

_____

_____

_____

_____

Question 2
Define *ambition*. Why can ambition be harmful to your maturity?

_____

_____

_____

_____

Question 3

According to Psalm 139:23-24 and Luke 15:17, how can we know when we've begun to mature?

_____

_____

_____

_____

Question 4

Read Deuteronomy 30:19-20, Ephesians 1:3, and 2 Corinthians 9:8. How has God given us the opportunity to be blessed?

_____

_____

_____

_____

Question 5

Think about the story about Jack Hayford and his dog. God heard his heart and wanted to bless Jack. Has there ever been a time when God blessed you in a similar way?

_____

_____

_____

_____

PRAY

If studying alone, ask the Holy Spirit to reveal the truth about Himself to you. If in a group, take some time to pray for each other as you think about the truths discussed in this session.

EXPLORE

Do you want to go deeper with this teaching? Here are some additional things to think about, pray for, or write about in your journal throughout the next week.

Key Quote

The act of blessing has nothing to do with you or your performance—it has to do with God's nature and who He is.

Why do you think God take such pleasure in blessing His children?

_____

_____

_____

_____

_____

Key Verses

Luke 15:12-13, 17, 19, 29, 31; Matthew 26:14-15; Philippians 2:3; Acts 8:19; Psalm 139:23-24

What truths stand out to you as you read these verses?

_____

_____

_____

What is the Holy Spirit saying to you through these Scriptures?

_____

_____

_____

Key Question
What stage are you in today? What do you need to do to mature into the next stage?

Key Prayer
Father God, thank You for all the blessings in my life right now. Even when things aren't perfect, help me see how You're working on my behalf. Lord Jesus, show me how to crucify my fleshly desires and completely trust You. I give You permission to come into my heart and do this work, as I cannot do it without You. Thank You for loving me. In Jesus' name, Amen.

4

BLESSED SONS AND DAUGHTERS

*God calls us to train our sons and daughters as children, teach them
when they are adolescents, and trust God with them when they are
adults.*

ENGAGE

As a child, did you have a hero or favorite role model? Who was it
and why?

WATCH

Watch "Blessed Sons and Daughters."
- Think about how godly discipline is loving.
- Look for how God's Word delineates children, teens, and
  adults, and how parents should relate to each.

(If you are not able to watch this teaching on video, read the
following. Otherwise, skip to the **Talk** section after viewing.)

READ

We are all sons and daughters of God. As sons and daughters, we all go through three phases that are outlined in the Bible. God designed these three phases, and I want to talk about how we relate to sons and daughters in each phase. The three phases are childhood, adolescence, and adulthood. Childhood is biblically defined as birth to 12 years old, adolescence age 13 to 19, and adulthood age 20 and above. I'm going to give you three words to help you remember how to relate to people in each of these three phases.

We're going to start with three verses from Ephesians 6, and I think these three verses give us each of the three phases of life.

> Children, obey your parents in the Lord, for this is right. "Honor your father and mother," which is the first commandment with promise: "that it may be well with you and you may live long on the earth" (v. 1-3).

Children first need to learn to obey. I think verse two refers to adolescents. Teenagers move on to a phase where they need to learn to honor each other and honor their parents. I believe that's the biggest thing teenagers need to learn.

Training

Ephesians 6:4 says, "And you, fathers, do not provoke your children to wrath, but bring them up in the training and admonition of the Lord." Think about Proverbs 22:6 that says,

Train up a child in the way he should go,
And when he is old he will not depart from it.

I'm going to talk about biblical training now, and I'm going to talk about spanking because the Bible talks about spanking. We have some friends who had read a book about not spanking and had decided to stop spanking in their home. A few weeks after they told us this, my wife, Debbie, spoke to them, and they said, "We've started spanking again." The bottom line is the Bible is the best book on raising children.

When my son was little, I'd tell him I was going to spank him because of a bad choice he'd made, and he'd say to me, "Daddy, can I just tell you something first?" Then he stared out into space for a while searching for something to say that would postpone the spanking. Eventually he'd say, "I love you, Daddy, and I have four dollars. I want to give you my four dollars, and that's not all. When I grow up I'm going to build you and Mommy a big house ..." And his speech went on and on. He did whatever he could to get out of the spanking, but he was never successful.

I'm going to read to you from the Message Bible now because I like how it translates this verse:

Don't be afraid to correct your young ones;
    a spanking won't kill them.
A good spanking, in fact, might save them
        from something worse than death (Proverbs 23:13–14 MSG).

The New King James Version says,

Do not withhold correction from a child,
For *if* you beat him with a rod, he will not die.
You shall beat him with a rod,
And deliver his soul from hell.

I have a choice: I can either listen to the parenting experts out there who don't know God or I can listen to God's Word, which says that spanking could deliver my child's soul from hell. The Bible is strong on this point, and we try to dilute it. Let me clarify now that when I'm talking about spanking, I'm not talking about spanking in anger, abuse, or anything like that. There's a whole message I did on this years ago, and you can go online to listen to that if you'd like. Many people think the Bible says, "Spare the rod, spoil the child." The Bible does not say that. The result is actually much worse. Here's what it actually says in Proverbs 13:24:

He who spares his rod hates his son,
but he who loves him disciplines him promptly.

Here are three things about discipline that might help you if you're in this phase of life:

1. Be Clear.

Be clear in your communication. I remember one time I walked out in the back yard, and my son James was throwing rocks into the swimming pool. I said, "James, do not throw any rocks into the swimming pool." He looked at me and then threw his brother's bicycle into the swimming pool. I didn't say not to throw bicycles into the pool. So I had to be clear: "Don't throw *anything* into the swimming pool. If you throw *anything*, including other people, into the pool, I'm going to spank you."

2. Be convincing.

"Daddy is going to spank you. Let me tell you why Daddy's going to spank you—because Daddy loves you. Bad things happen to people who do bad things. I don't want bad things to happen to you, so I am training you now not to do bad things. If you do bad things when you're older, you'll go to prison."

3. Be compassionate.

Never spank in anger. If you have to cool down first, do it. Explain to them why they're being spanked. Take them to another room and never spank them in public, because that is shaming. Shame is never a part of discipline with God. He never shames us. Have fun with them after the discipline is over. Show them when the discipline time has ended. It's important for them to know when it's over. It takes time for godly discipline.

Teaching

This phase refers to adolescence. From age 13–19, we move from training to teaching. Let's take a look at Ephesians 6:4: "And you, fathers, do not provoke your children to wrath, but bring them up in the training and admonition of the Lord." I used the word teaching because *admonition* means instruction or teaching.

Deuteronomy 4:9 says, "And teach them [statutes] to your children and your grandchildren." Deuteronomy 6:7 says, "You shall teach them diligently to your children, and shall talk of them when you sit in your house, when you walk by the way, when you lie down, and when you rise up."

Think about this. Adolescence refers to the transition of a child becoming an adult. We see this change happen in Jesus' life. Look in Luke 2:42 and notice something Jesus did in his transition from childhood to adolescence. Luke 2:42, 46 say, "And when He was twelve years old, they went up to Jerusalem according to the custom of the feast ... Now so it was that after three days they found Him in the temple, sitting in the midst of the teachers, both listening to them and asking them questions."

This is a time when teenagers are going to begin to ask questions, and you need to understand something: this is the time for you to help them transition from being a child. Many times you'll hear teenagers say, "You're treating me like a child," and of course we respond, "Because you're acting like a child." But it's our responsibility to teach them not to act like children any longer. In other words, we tell/train a child what to think, but we teach an adolescent how to think.

This is like learning math. Some people were never able to learn math well because they were taught the answers but not the processes (or how to get to the answer). My father, a mathematical genius, taught me mathematical processes and often showed me how to solve problems three or four different ways. This is what's wrong sometimes with teenagers—we tell them what they're going to do instead of teaching them how to come to that conclusion on their own.

When in the temple, Jesus was asking questions. The best way to teach, if you don't know this already, is to ask questions. So in this time of transition, you as the parent will begin to ask them questions instead of telling them what to do. For example, you could ask, "What kind of criteria are you going to use when you choose your friends?" "What type of study habits are you going to develop now that are going to help you later in life?" And here's a question I wish someone would've asked me when I was growing up: "Do you think the choices you make now will affect you as an adult?"

When our children were making the transition to adolescence and turning thirteen, we had a covenant ceremony with each of them. I did it with the boys, and Debbie did it with our daughter. We took them on an overnight trip, gave them a ring, and talked about many things. Just as an example, we talked about dating. We talked about the facts of life with them when they were 10 and 13.

The reason we did it when they turned 10 was because they were going to learn about it at school. We'd say, "There are some things you need to understand. You're going to begin to be attracted to the opposite sex. And when that happens, we want to tell you about changes that are going to happen in your body and emotions. We want to make a covenant with you. You have a part, and we have a part. Your part is talking to us and being open and honest with us when you're attracted to someone; that you'll keep yourself pure and not cross the boundaries God has set in place for your protection before marriage. My part of the covenant is that I commit to pray with you about your spouse because we know you better than anyone else in the world knows you. (It's crucial you tell teenagers why.) We know your personality and giftings. So we're going to help you in this process." I personally wanted to give them an incentive, so part of my covenant was that I'd pay for wedding expenses, honeymoon, college, and help them buy their first house. I look back on that now and think, "Thank God people buy my books because I'd never have been able to keep the promises I made!"

When my oldest son, Josh, turned 13, I wanted to teach him something about grace. I told him, "We've made this covenant. What's going to happen if you don't do your part?" I was expecting him to say, "If I don't do my part, you won't do yours." But my 13-year-old son surprised me. He sat, thinking for moment, and then said, "You'll probably still do your part." I remember thinking, "He stole my thunder!" So I said, "Well, if you don't do your part, why do you think I'll do my part?" He told me, "Because you've taught us that even when we do things wrong, God still loves us. And I think you're like God, Dad."

Trusting

The last phase is adulthood. Children are trained. Teenagers are taught. Adults are trusted.

Adulthood in the Bible starts at twenty years old. Exodus 30:14 says that at age 20, they began to give offerings. It's good to teach our children to give offerings, but this passage is actually referring to a temple tax they were required to start paying at age 20. Numbers 1:3 says they didn't have to go to war until age 20. Numbers 14:29-32 says that beginning at age 20, they were held responsible for their sin. He said, "Your little ones who have no knowledge of good and evil will still go into the Promised Land, but everyone twenty years old and up, other than Joshua and Caleb, will die in the wilderness."

God sets the age of adulthood at 20. Some people believe that once people are married, they're adults. They base this on the verse that says, "Therefore a man shall leave his father and mother and cleave to his wife." In other words, "They're under my authority until they get married." No. Take the scripture for what it says—"Therefore, a man ..." It doesn't say a boy. When a man gets married, he's already a man and no longer a boy. Marriage doesn't make him a man. Think about this: what if they never get married? Some people are not called to marriage but to celibacy. Jesus even talked about that Himself.

At age 20, they're grown and need to be treated as adults. This is the reason I entitled this message "Blessed Sons and Daughters," not Blessed Children. I'm calling them adult sons and daughters. I don't even like calling them adult children—that's an oxymoron. Think about it—if they're adults, they're not children. We encounter many problems when we don't understand this.

Parents get in the way sometimes when God's trying to do something in an adult's life. Recall the story of Samson. Debbie and I were just in Israel, and I saw the place where Samson was born and where his tomb is now. I saw the hill of Timnah where he fell in love with the Philistine woman and wanted to marry her and his parents didn't want him to. I want you to notice a verse that a lot of people miss. Judges 14:4 says, "But his father and mother did not know that it was of the Lord—that He was seeking an occasion to move against the Philistines. For at that time the Philistines had dominion over Israel." This was before Delilah, by the way. Here's what I think was happening. I think God was trying to teach Samson something, because Samson ended up marrying another Philistine woman named Delilah and lost the anointing of God. His parents didn't know what God's will was.

So many times we feel we still have to parent our adult sons and daughters. It's hard not to step in unsolicited or want to give firmer advice than we should. Debbie and I have had to help each other with this and remind each other they're adults—our parenting role is over.

The word *parent* can be a noun or a verb. In other words, yes, I am a parent, but I do not parent anymore, because I don't have children anymore—I have adult sons and daughters. You might not have ever thought about this: my sons and daughters are now my brothers and sisters (in Christ). They're not my kids anymore. They're now my friends. They can come to me for advice, but really they're coming to a brother in Christ. Some sons and daughters won't go to their parents for advice anymore, for two reasons:

1. Sometimes parents try to control. They think their sons or daughters aren't honoring them if they don't take their advice. Some parents even quote Scripture to try to get their sons or daughters to do what they think they should do. That is spiritual abuse. Once your children are grown, you don't have authority in their lives.

2. Sometimes there actually is a dishonoring because you ought to honor parents and ask for their counsel. It doesn't mean you have to do what they suggest. You have to hear God. I've heard of some people deciding they were going to move away or make a big change and just announcing it to their parents, instead of asking for their advice. That is dishonoring. The reason they do it is because they haven't made the transition from adolescence to adulthood yet, and they don't have the courage to say, "Would you pray with us about this?" They're afraid the parents will say not to do it. They don't have the courage to say, "Well, we heard God differ-

ently, so we'll pray about it again." They don't have courage
to say, "We appreciate your counsel, but we prayed again,
and we know for sure this is what God has spoken to us." It
would solve about 90% of family/marriage counseling issues
if we treated our sons and daughters as brothers and sisters
and let them grow up.

I want to show you a Scripture about this that's frequently
misunderstood. Contextually in this passage, Jesus is rebuking the
Pharisees for spiritual abuse. Matthew 23:8-10 says,

> But you, do not be called 'Rabbi;' for One is your Teacher, the
> Christ, and you are all brethren. Do not call anyone on earth your
> father; for One is your Father, He who is in heaven. And do not be
> called teachers; for One is your Teacher, the Christ.

We can see the Trinity in these verses. The Pharisees loved
titles and loved to abuse the authority that came with titles.
Jesus was saying, "If you're going to say that because you have
a title, you have authority over a person, you need to know the
Ones Who have authority are the Holy Spirit, the Father, and
the Son. And you're all brothers." No matter what age someone
is, when that person becomes an adult, you're now his brother
in Christ.

I was meeting with my counselor one time, and he said, "Do
you remember a time when you were welcomed into manhood?"

I did, and I told him about it. When I went away to college, my father gave me his credit card to pay for meals. Then when I went on my honeymoon, he told me to put all our expenses on the credit card. At this time, I worked for my father who owned the company. He asked me to come to his office when I got back Monday morning. He asked if we had a good trip and if we'd put everything on the credit card. I said yes. Then he asked me to stand up, so I stood. He asked me to give him back his credit card, so I gave it to him, and he put it back in his wallet. He then put his hand out to shake mine and said, "Congratulations, son. You are now a man. You need to provide for your family from now on, like I provided for you. And you need to lead your family spiritually like I led you."

That's what a lot of young men need today. If you haven't heard it from a biological father, then hear it from a spiritual father. The last words of David to Solomon were, "Be strong and prove that you're a man." That didn't mean the world's definition of a man, but for Solomon to love God with all his heart, mind, soul, and strength.

God is a generational God—He named Himself the God of Abraham, Isaac, and Jacob. A little over a year ago, my son Josh came to me asking counsel for something that was in his heart— to start a church. My plan was that he would succeed me as pastor of Gateway Church. But I told him I released him from that, and now he's in Austin planting a church there. Two weeks ago, he preached here and did a great job feeding God's sheep. I could recognize 10 things he was doing well. I sat and watched my son feed the congregation God's Word, thinking about the plans I had made for the church. Then I had two thoughts. The first thought was, "He messed up my plan!" But my second thought was, "I trust my son because I raised him to be a man of God and now he's following God."

NOTES

_____

_____

_____

_____

_____

_____

TALK

These questions can be used for group discussion or personal reflection.

Question 1

According to Proverbs 13:24 and 23:13-14, what does God's Word say about disciplining our children?

_____

_____

_____

_____

Question 2

What are three ways our discipline can be godly and loving?

_____

_____

_____

_____

Question 3

Read Luke 2:42 and Deuteronomy 4:9. How should our relationship and responsibility to our children change when they become teenagers?

_____

_____

_____

_____

Question 4

What is one reason adult sons and daughters no longer ask their parents for advice? As parents of adult sons and daughters, how can we honor them?

_____

_____

_____

_____

Question 5

According to Jesus in Matthew 23:8-10, how should we relate to
our grown sons and daughters?

_____

_____

_____

_____

PRAY

If studying alone, ask the Holy Spirit to reveal the truth about Himself to you. If in a group, take some time to pray for each other as you think about the truths discussed in this session.

EXPLORE

Do you want to go deeper with this teaching? Here are some additional things to think about, pray for, or write about in your journal throughout the next week.

Key Quote

> *No matter what age someone is, when that person becomes an adult, you're now his brother in Christ.*

How would you treat someone who is your brother in Christ differently than you would treat your child?

_____

_____

_____

_____

_____

Key Verses

Ephesians 6:1-4; Proverbs 13:24; 23:13-14; Matthew 23:8-10

What truths stand out to you as you read these verses?

_____

_____

_____

What is the Holy Spirit saying to you through these Scriptures?

_____

_____

_____

Key Question

How can we pray for our children, no matter what age?

Key Prayer

Father God, thank You for being such a kind, loving Father. Thank You for showing me the truth in Your Word and giving me a strong foundation on which to build my family. Holy Spirit, please walk with me every minute of every day and guide me. And when my children have grown, help me release them to You and trust that You are constantly working in their lives for their good. In Jesus' name, Amen.

5

THE FAMILY OF GOD

When we are saved, we're reborn and adopted into a new family of love, favor, and blessings.

ENGAGE

If you could meet any biblical character, whom would it be, and why?

WATCH

Watch "The Family of God."

- Think about what it means to be a member of the family of God.
- Look for the differences between the family you were born into and God's family.

(If you are not able to watch this teaching on video, read the following. Otherwise, skip to the **Talk** section after viewing.)

READ

We've been in a series called "Blessed Families," and I couldn't leave this subject without talking about the ultimate blessed family—the family of God. By God's grace, we've all become a part of this family. We were raised in another family—not your biological family, but a spiritual family. We were born in the family of Adam and Eve after the Fall, and now we've been born again into the family of God.

Think about Moses. He was born a Hebrew but raised in an Egyptian family. He didn't know God. Hebrews 11 speaks of how Moses chose not to associate with his Egyptian family after he found out he was born a Hebrew because they didn't know God and worshipped many pagan gods and idols. Moses had to retrain himself.

I didn't get saved until I was 19 years old. For 19 years I belonged to the world's family, even though I grew up in a Christian home. Then I came to Christ and found out I belonged to a new family.

Ephesians 2:19 says, "Now, therefore, you are no longer strangers and foreigners, but fellow citizens with the saints and members of the household of God." This word *household* refers to family, and the passage is speaking to Gentiles. You are now members of the family of God. Ephesians 3:14-15 says, "For this reason I bow my knees to the Father of our Lord Jesus Christ, from whom the whole family in heaven and earth is named."

We got our name from Christ—we're called Christians. The word *Christian* means "Christ-like." We now have the name of God! It's similar to when you marry into a family and your last name changes.

When our two sons and daughter got married, we talked with their future spouses before their marriage and told them they were marrying into a family with a name that's associated with the kingdom. There were some things we wanted them to understand now that they were going to be associated with our family. One of them brought up a story about my son, Josh. About 10 years ago, he worked in our media department. One morning, he was late and driving too fast, so he got pulled over by a police officer. The officer asked him, "Do you have any reason for driving fast this morning?" Josh replied, "Well, it's not a good reason, but I'm late for work." The officer asked where he worked, and Josh told him, "Gateway Church." The officer looked down at Josh's driver's license, saw his last name, said, "Aw man, I can't give my pastor's son a ticket!" So when we had these talks with our kids' future spouses, they'd joke and ask, "Does this mean I get out of speeding tickets now?"

Here's what it means to marry into the family of God:

Born into a Family of Unconditional Love

When you get saved, you are born into a family of unconditional love from God and others. The "others" are our brothers and sisters in Christ, and they're still human. There are times when brothers and sisters in Christ don't act out of unconditional love, but there's

never a time that your Father doesn't. Your Father loves you unconditionally. It took years for me to understand this truth. The world's
love is conditional, performance-based love. But the love within the
kingdom of God is unconditional.

John 3:16 says, "For God so loved the world that He gave His
only begotten Son, that whoever believes in Him should not perish
but have everlasting life." That's unconditional love! Romans 5:8
says it another way, "But God demonstrates His own love toward
us, in that while we were still sinners, Christ died for us." God
didn't wait to see if you'd behave perfectly before He gave His Son
as a sacrifice for you. He gave His Son while we were still sinners
mocking Him, spitting on Him, and nailing Him to a cross. You can
never do anything that would cause God not to love you. Romans 8
says *nothing* can ever separate us from the love of God. You can't
blow it bad enough for God not to love you.

I taught our children a little expression when they were young.
I'd ask them, "How does Daddy love you?" And they'd answer,
"With all his heart, no matter what, forever and always." And then
I'd say, "And how does God love you?" The answer was the same,
"With all His heart, no matter what, forever and always." This
would change our lives if we could truly know it in our hearts.

There's a verse in Luke 6 that's one of my favorites. Verse 35
says, "For He is kind to the unthankful and evil." Before an image of
someone comes to your mind, look in the mirror. I know I personally haven't always been thankful, and I haven't always done the
right thing. But God has always been kind.

One day, I had a friend come to me for counsel regarding his son. His son was failing out of college, and my friend had just received a call that his son was in jail for many unpaid parking tickets. My friend said, "I'm thinking about getting him out of jail, taking him back to college, and taking his car away until he pays all the parking tickets. I feel like it's time for some tough love." There are times for tough love, but I got a sense that this was a time for unconditional love. I told my friend, "I think you ought to go pick him up, pay all his fines and tickets, take him home with you, and tell him, 'Everything's paid in full. You never have to pay me back for it, and I feel like there's something going on your life right now and I haven't been listening to you. I'd like to ask you to forgive me for not listening to your heart, and I'd like for us to talk about what is in your heart.'" He did this, and his son started crying. His son said, "I feel like you're pushing me in a direction, and I don't know what to do." His dad asked him what he wanted to do. His dad traveled a lot running presidential campaigns for Central and South America, and the son asked if he could travel with him for a while. After a few months, the son told his dad, "I know what I want to do—I'd like to do what you do, but I need to go back to college for that." He went back and got a bachelor's and a master's degree and went to work with his dad. His attitude had completely changed.

I know there are times for tough love, but there are also times to say, "Your debt's been paid. I love you, and I want to rebuild our relationship."

Adopted into a Family of Unmerited Favor

We're adopted into a family of unmerited favor. That's the definition of *grace*—unmerited favor. Ephesians 1:5 says, " Having predestined us to adoption as sons by Jesus Christ to Himself." Galatians 4:6-7 says:

> And because you are sons, God has sent forth the Spirit of His Son into your hearts, crying out, "Abba, Father!" Therefore you are no longer a slave but a son, and if a son, then an heir of God through Christ.

The first time the Bible mentions the phrase "Abba Father" is in the Gospel of Mark. *Abba* is the Aramaic word for father. Jesus spoke Aramaic. The three languages of His day were Hebrew, Aramaic, and Greek. Most of the time, Greek was used for writing; the Bible's New Testament was written in Greek. About a fifth of Jewish people in that day spoke in Hebrew, but the spoken language for most people at that time was Aramaic. *Father* in this Greek passage means "The Father." Jesus said, in the language He spoke, "Father, The Father." I think He was saying, "You're not only The Father, You're My Father." He was making it very personal. Then Paul, writing in Galatians and Romans, says we can now also call Him Father.

Second Corinthians 6:18 says,

> "I will be a Father to you,
> And you shall be My sons and daughters,
> says the Lord Almighty."

Have you ever understood that you're a son or daughter of God—that God is your Father? I know it's difficult for some of you because you had a bad father. I'm so sorry about that, and we'll talk about that in a moment. But the true Father—a loving, protective, providing, giving, and unconditionally loving father who holds the world together in His hands—is your Father!

I grew up with a good father. My father owned a company, and I worked for that company but never really saw myself as an employee because I was the owner's son. My name was on the building too. I didn't get paid like he did, but I still knew who my father was. During my college years, I worked for my Dad over the summers. One summer, I came back, and there was a new foreman working there in the job site trailer. Most of the men working there knew I was the owner's son, but this foreman did not know me yet. We sat one day in the trailer having lunch, and when my Dad drove up, the foreman said, "Well, here comes Mr. Big." I probably shouldn't have, but I said, "So, who's Mr. Big?" He replied, "Oh, J.P.—Mr. Morris. He owns the company and thinks he runs things around here, but actually I'm the one who runs things around here." I said, "Oh, that's good to know." Then my Dad stuck his head in the door and said hi to everyone and then asked me, "Hey son, since it's your first day back from college, I was wondering if you'd like to go to lunch?" I said, "I'd love to ... Dad." Have you ever watched color drain from someone's face? I told the foreman later, "You might call him Mr. Big—I call him Dad." He was really nice to me the rest of the summer.

Listen—your Dad is more than the owner of the company. He owns the world, the universe, and all that dwells therein! He owns it all—that's your Dad!

This might shock you though: you might not know who your dad was before you got saved. Satan was your spiritual dad before you got saved. Jesus tells us this in John 8:38-39:

> "I speak what I have seen with My Father, and you do what you have seen with your father. They answered and said to Him, 'Abraham is our father.' Jesus said to them, 'If you were Abraham's children, you would do the works of Abraham."

The works of Abraham are to believe in Jesus. Abraham believed God, and it was accounted to him as righteousness—he believed Jesus, the Son of Man, who came and met with him and told him his wife would have a son in her old age. Jesus goes on to say:

> "But now you seek to kill Me, a Man who has told you the truth which I heard from God. Abraham did not do this. You do the deeds of your father." Then they said to Him, "We were not born of fornication; we have one Father—God." Jesus said to them, "If God were your Father, you would love Me ... You are of your father the devil" (John 8:40-42, 44).

For 19 years, my spiritual father (not my earthly father) was Satan. He was abusive and angry—a tormentor and an accuser. If you were born in a bad family, you need to know everything bad that ever happened to you was Satan. Even if you were born in a good family, everything bad that ever happened to you was Satan. Same father. All your anger, fear, insecurity, inferiority, rejection, guilt, and impurity were all from your old spiritual father. But you now have a good Father who's adopted you into a good family.

We have some friends who adopted a girl from another country. She was older when they adopted her. When they brought her home, she was surprised to have her own room, having lived in an orphanage. A few months after she'd been living with them, they discovered that when they cleared the dinner table at night, she was hiding food in her room. She didn't know if there would be food the next day. Then they bought her some nice clothes, and the girl hid her new dress under her mattress, afraid someone would steal it. She'd been living in a different family, and it took her a long time to get used to the new family. That's how it is when we get saved.

Transferred into a Family of Unearned Blessings

When we get saved, we're transferred into a family of unearned blessings. Colossians 1:13 says, "For he has rescued us from the kingdom of darkness and transferred us into the Kingdom of his dear Son" (NLT). He's transferred us from the family of darkness to the family of His Son. It's a family of blessing. The first thing God did after creating Adam and Eve was bless them. Genesis 1:28 says, "Then God blessed them." Then, after the Fall, the first thing God did was let them know the curses they had brought on themselves.

The last word of the last sentence of the last chapter of the last book of the Old Testament is "cursed." The first word in the first sentence of the first sermon in the New Testament is "blessed." Jesus came to remove the curse.

Galatians 3:13-14 says it this way:

> Christ has redeemed us from the curse of the law, having become a curse for us (for it is written, "Cursed *is* everyone who hangs on a tree"), that the blessing of Abraham might come upon the Gentiles in Christ Jesus, that we might receive the promise of the Spirit through faith.

The blessing of Abraham was to leave his family and go to the land flowing with milk and honey. Part of the curse was that the land wasn't going to produce. It's amazing to go to Israel and see the desert surrounding it, but Israel itself is so fertile because the land isn't cursed anymore. You still have to plant seed and water it, but it's not cursed.

You are not living in a cursed family anymore, but a blessed one. And God is your Father. He adopted you into this new family. You didn't earn it, but He blesses you.

Psalm 68:6 says, "God places the lonely in families." No matter what kind of family you came from, how young or old you are, or what your marital status is, you belong to a new family now. You never have to be lonely again because God has given you a new family.

In adoption, the parents adopt the children—the children don't adopt the parents. You did not adopt God into your life—He adopted you. By the way, you didn't choose God either—you chose to believe, but He chose you long before you believed. Here's what happened: God came to the adoption agency, the orphanage of the world, and pointed down at you and said, "I want that child right there." Satan would've said something like this, "Oh, sorry, you can't have that child right there—he's mine." And God said, "But I want that one." You were that child. God knew what kind of a father Satan was and that he abused you. Satan probably said something like this: "Okay, you want that child? I'll give you that child if you'll give me Your Little Boy. But just so we're clear about this, let me tell You what I'm going to do to Your Son. I'm going to beat Him, spit on Him, and nail Him to a cross until He dies. Now, do you still want this child?" Our Father said, "Yes." And now you're in a new family.

NOTES

_____

_____

_____

_____

_____

TALK

These questions can be used for group discussion or personal reflection.

Question 1

What were you previously taught about God's love? Did you have to earn it? Could you lose it?

_____

_____

_____

_____

Question 2

Is it difficult for you to imagine God as a good, loving Father? How is Father God different from your earthly biological father?

_____

_____

_____

_____

Question 3

Like the story of the adopted orphan girl who hid her new dress under her bed, what spiritual concepts were hard for you to accept when you were a new Christian?

_____

_____

_____

_____

Question 4

How have you seen the blessings of God on your life since you've been saved? What has changed?

_____

_____

_____

_____

Question 5

How do you think someone would live life differently if they under-stood that they are completely and unconditionally loved by their heavenly Father?

_____

_____

_____

_____

PRAY

If studying alone, ask the Holy Spirit to reveal the truth about Himself to you. If in a group, take some time to pray for each other as you think about the truths discussed in this session.

EXPLORE

Do you want to go deeper with this teaching? Here are some additional things to think about, pray for, or write about in your journal throughout the next week.

Key Quote

You can never do anything that would cause God not to love you.

Why do you think people struggle with the concept of God's unconditional love?

_____

_____

_____

_____

_____

Key Verses

Ephesians 1:5; 2:1; 3:14-15; Romans 5:8; Galatians 3:13-14; 4:6-7; 2
Corinthians 6:18; John 3:16, 8:38-44; Colossians 1:13; Genesis 1:28

What truths stand out to you as you read these verses?

_____

_____

_____

What is the Holy Spirit saying to you through these Scriptures?

_____

_____

_____

Key Question

How does knowing you have a new, eternal family affect your
everyday relationships?

Key Prayer

Heavenly Father, thank. You for making me part of Your family.
Help me deepen my understanding of what it means to be Your
child. Jesus, thank You for taking my place on the cross so I could
be the benefactor of these immense blessings and freedom. Holy
Spirit, continue to grow the knowledge of Your love deep in my
heart, and may my thoughts, beliefs, and actions reflect that I am a
beloved child of God. In Jesus' name I pray these things. Amen.

LEADER'S GUIDE

The *Blessed Families* Leader's Guide is designed to help you lead your small group or class through the *Blessed Families* curriculum. Use this guide along with the curriculum for a life-changing, interactive experience.

BEFORE YOU MEET

- Ask God to prepare the hearts and minds of the people in your group. Ask Him to show you how to encourage each person to integrate the principles all of you discover into your daily lives through group discussion and writing in your journals.
- Preview the video segment for the week.
- Plan how much time you'll give to each portion of your meeting (see the suggested schedule below). In case you're unable to get through all of the activities in the time you have planned, here is a list of the most important questions (from the **Talk** section) for each week.

SUGGESTED SMALL GROUP SCHEDULE

1. **Engage** and **Recap** (5 Minutes)
2. **Watch** or **Read** (20 Minutes)
3. **Talk** (25 Minutes)
4. **Pray** (10 minutes)

SESSION ONE

Q: If Jesus came to redeem us from the curse of sin, why do some people continue to live under that curse?

Q: What lie did Adam and Eve believe when they chose to sin and eat the forbidden fruit? What was the truth?

SESSION TWO

Q: In Matthew 19, how does Jesus respond to the Pharisees' question?

Q: How can marriage attract or repel unbelievers when it comes to Christ?

SESSION THREE

Q: According to Psalm 139:23-24 and Luke 15:17, how can we know when we've begun to mature?

Q: Read Deuteronomy 30:19-20, Ephesians 1:3, and 2 Corinthians 9:8. How has God given us the opportunity to be blessed?

SESSION FOUR

Q: According to Proverbs 13:24 and 23:13-14, what does God's Word say about disciplining our children?

Q: Read Luke 2:42 and Deuteronomy 4:9. How should our relationship and responsibility to our children change when they become teenagers?

SESSION FIVE

Q: What were you previously taught about God's love? Did you have to earn it? Could you lose it?

Q: How do you think someone would live life differently if they understood that they are completely and unconditionally loved by their heavenly Father?

Remember, the goal is not necessarily to get through all of the questions. The highest priority is for the group to learn and engage in a dynamic discussion.

HOW TO USE THE CURRICULUM

This study has a simple design.

The One Thing

This is a brief statement under each session title that sums up the main point—the key idea—of the session.

Recap

Recap the previous week's session, inviting members to share about any opportunities they have encountered throughout the week that apply to what they learned (this doesn't apply to the first week).

Engage

Ask the icebreaker question to help get people talking and feeling comfortable with one another.

Watch

Watch the videos (recommended).

Read

If you're unable to watch the videos, read these sections.

Talk

The questions in these lessons are intentionally open-ended. Use them to help the group members reflect on Scripture and the lesson.

Pray

Ask members to share their concerns and then pray together. Be sensitive to the Holy Spirit and the needs of the group.

Explore

Encourage members to complete the written portion in their books before the next meeting.

KEY TIPS FOR THE LEADER

- Generate participation and discussion.
- Resist the urge to teach. The goal is for great conversation that leads to discovery.
- Ask open-ended questions—questions that can't be answered with "yes" or "no" (e.g., "What do you think about that?" rather than "Do you agree?")
- When a question arises, ask the group for their input first, instead of immediately answering it yourself.
- Be comfortable with silence. If you ask a question and no one responds, rephrase the question and wait for a response. Your primary role is to create an environment where people feel comfortable to be themselves and participate, not to provide the answers to all of their questions.
- Ask the group to pray for each other from week to week, especially about key issues that arise during your group time. This is how you begin to build authentic community and encourage spiritual growth within the group.

KEYS TO A DYNAMIC SMALL GROUP

Relationships

Meaningful, encouraging relationships are the foundation of a dynamic small group. Teaching, discussion, worship, and prayer are important elements of a group meeting, but the depth of each element is often dependent upon the depth of the relationships among members.

Availability

Building a sense of community within your group requires members to prioritize their relationships with one another. This means being available to listen, care for one another, and meet each other's needs.

Mutual Respect

Mutual respect is shown when members value each other's opinions (even when they disagree) and are careful never to put down or embarrass others in the group (including their spouses, who may or may not be present).

Openness

A healthy small group environment encourages sincerity and transparency. Members treat each other with grace in areas of weakness, allowing each other room to grow.

Confidentiality

To develop authenticity and a sense of safety within the group, each member must be able to trust that things discussed within the group will not be shared outside the group.

Shared Responsibility
Group members will share the responsibility of group meetings by using their God-given abilities to serve at each gathering. Some may greet, some may host, some may teach, etc. Ideally, each person should be available to care for others as needed.

Sensitivity
Dynamic small groups are born when the leader consistently seeks and is responsive to the guidance of the Holy Spirit, following His leading throughout the meeting as opposed to sticking to the "agenda." This guidance is especially important during the discussion and ministry time.

Fun!
Dynamic small groups take the time to have fun. Create an atmosphere for fun and be willing to laugh at yourself every now and then!

ABOUT THE AUTHOR

Robert Morris is the lead senior pastor of Gateway Church, a multicampus church in the Dallas/Fort Worth Metroplex. Since it began in 2000, the church has grown to more than 39,000 active members. His television program is aired in over 190 countries, and his radio feature, *Worship & the Word with Pastor Robert,* airs on radio stations across America. He serves as chancellor of The King's University and is the bestselling author of 15 books including *The Blessed Life, Truly Free, Frequency,* and *Beyond Blessed.* Robert and his wife, Debbie, have been married 38 years and are blessed with one married daughter, two married sons, and nine grandchildren. He lives in Dallas, TX.

More resources for your small group by Pastor Robert Morris!

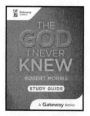

Study Guide: 978-1-945529-54-2
DVD: 978-1-949399-41-7

Study Guide: 978-1-949399-54-7
DVD: 978-1-949399-51-6

Study Guide: 978-1-945529-51-1
DVD: 978-1-949399-49-3

Study Guide: 978-1-945529-71-9
DVD: 978-1-949399-50-9

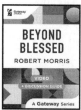

DVD + Discussion Guide:
978-1-949399-68-4

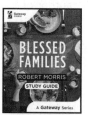

Study Guide: 978-1-949399-55-4
DVD: 978-1-949399-52-3

Study Guide: 978-1-945529-85-6
DVD: 978-1-949399-48-6

Study Guide: 978-1-945529-56-6
DVD: 978-1-949399-43-1

Study Guide: 978-1-945529-55-9
DVD: 978-1-949399-42-4

Study Guide: 978-1-945529-88-7
DVD: 978-1-949399-53-0

Study Guide: 978-1-949399-65-3
DVD: 978-1-949399-66-0

Study Guide: 978-0-997429-84-8
DVD: 978-1-949399-46-2

You can find these resources and others at
www.gatewaypublishing.com